Esquire Publications
1400 Highway 41 N., #2503
Inverness, FL 34451
www.esquirepublications.com
Tel: 1-800-501-7640

"Rhymes to Rhythms"

Edited By: Georgia Editing Service, LLC.
Book and Cover Design By
Designs Unparallel, LLC
www.designsunparallel.net

Library of Congress Cataloging-in-Publication Data
Library of Congress Control Number: 2021906017
ISBN: 9781513683706

32.2012

Every sequel is done well
When done in 4 years spell
Been working on this dream 28 years strong
Doing what I can to see right from wrong
Now I'm down to the wire
Been through rain, snow, and fire

To get there is my ultimate goal
Seems like I sold my soul
Dreams of only sweet retire
Just like the sun rolling, great ball of fire
How will I know just count 1- 4?
Take it or leave it, I want no more

The opening take is long gone
The first of 4 is just begun
3 to go to make 32
Not feeling old, but brand new
Like a baptism in the scheme of things
Come 32 I'm over the rims

A Universon

I'm not one person I'm many I'm a universon
Out of many one people one person
No one practice that version
Not too late to be a world champion
A world citizen and a bastion
Let the bells of freedom rein
Let the politicians sponsor their freedom train
Not too late what we can gain
Some of us on the brink of going insane

I'm not one person, I'm many, I'm a universon
Out of many, one people, one person
No one practice that version

We see what these times can bring
I don't profess to know everything
But I see with my own eyes
It's death before dishonor or everyone dies

I'm not one person, I'm many, I'm a universon
Out of many one people one person
No one practice that version

I've seen their scary games
They know in time who to blame
But as it is engraved in our destiny
The majority will end up seriously the minority

Alibi

Today I spoke to my alibi
Gorgeous pretty little baby cry
"Hola!"
"Ese es mi Da Da"
"Si mi amor"
Then she says, no more

Time and distance separate us
Train, car, maybe by bus
I might get there from time to time
Living this way may seem a crime
But it's my last gift to the living light
One day I must make it right

Sit tight the time is nigh
I really wanna hear my baby cry
One day she might validate me
Time and space may not agree
But all that matters is true
Will be here to see her through

Anchor

My name is Anchor
Born and bred in Grange Hill Jamaica
Son of a Welder
And a Bartender
Flunked out in high school
Did not learn the golden rule

No wife that I should care for
No child near or far
Just me, myself, and I
After my father die
I lost my mother
Now just the brother

Who cares for me?
He is father, mother, and brother you see
He brings me clothes and gives me money
He makes sure I am never hungry
But I am always drinking
And multiple drug using

That makes him very sad
Sometimes very mad
But I can't drop this monkey
That's all that make me happy
Till death do us part
I can't change this crooked heart

In Grange Hill I live like a king
No work, no bills, no nothing
Compliments of my brother
Who bails me out when I falter
So, life goes on crooked heartbroken mind
Until I reach the end of the line

At The Laundromat

Every tic and every toc of the universal clock
Tells me I've lost another sock
Somewhere in this large machine
Lurks a black hole grim and mean

Which devours hosiery
What is all of this to me?
Somewhere in my Frigidaire
I shall find another pair

DANVILLE TARDIEL

Backyard Recipes

All pure all organic veggies
All pure backyard recipes
Grown from fertile soil
A little water a little toil

Curry, stew, any style
Food on the table all the time
Concocted backyard recipes
Mouthwatering tasty entrees

We all wait for summer to come
To plant our seeds in shiny sun
Then we wait a few more days
To see and taste the beauty of our ways

Bashment

Don't bash me because of my age
Don't bash me you don't know what I crave
Don't bash me don't put me in the grave
Just get out the way and let the music play

In younger years I've learned to listen
With age now I know what's missing
Wisdom grows only time can tell
Time goes by you creep out of your shell

Don't bash me because of my age
Don't bash me you don't know what I crave
Don't bash me don't put me in the grave
Just get out the way and let the music play

In this life this sweet old life
Living through much strain and strife
Sometimes your best day is hard to remember
Come what may hold on and never surrender

Don't bash me because of my age
Don't bash me you don't know what I crave
Don't bash me don't put me in the grave
Just get out the way and let the music play

Big Brother

I was 14 years old when I first met you,
And I remember thinking, he seems unfriendly.
One year later, I learned something new,
You were full of jokes, the life of the party.
I also found out about your many talents,
Including the delicious food, you cooked to satisfy our palates.
My mom always loved how you cleaned clothes
Because you made her whites look like fresh snow.
And I always loved how you had my back,
I never had a sibling to look out for me like that.
We almost shared the same birthday too
Exactly one month apart, me before you.
You were one of the bravest people I knew,
The fact that you were taken from us is cruel.
You always said you "never feared death because everyone has their time,"
Well, your time was far too soon and the way you left is considered a crime.
But now you get to see your mother's face,
And you are both resting in a better place.
Now here I stand at 22,
I want to thank you for all the years you were true,
To me, my mom, and my dad,
You were the best big brother I ever had.

———

Brother

Brother, brother
Many, many years since we know each other
It was like yesterday
As kids we play
Marbles and things
In the backyard and rings

Throughout the years
Of chores and tears
One parent present
Watches without relent
Bought us toys even minibus
Now he's gone leaving just the two of us

I got stronger as time goes on
Will last longer 'cause I belong
True to the fruit of the vine
That brought us here in time
Your weight is nothing on our journey
We will end this in total harmony

DANVILLE TARDIEL

Much love to you my brother
Love is what keep us together
Live your live as you see right
No fuss and surely no fight
One day when the time is right
We will take off on our final flight

———

Child Of Adversity

Sound and strong is the mind of man
In the face of adversity, it moves on
Searching for a place a common ground
A peaceful comfort no one else around

Through the lightning storms tattered and torn
A special one gifted and wise, a hero is born
The winds of change blow strong and hard
The tides drift, the patterns change, we drop our guard

The pendulum swings
Changing all things
Yet one grows steady in mind and body
A flicker of hope in all adversity

Daughter

Daughter of mine my continuity
In the passage of time, you inherit me
In the links of life or a blink in time
Father, mother, daughter sublime

The passage of genes overwhelmingly true
Ninety-nine-point nine percent of me is you
Your hair, your eyes, your radiant hue
Everything and more I see in you

Your brain your level of intelligence
Never did I dream of such competence
You make me happy to spend time with you
That's when I know I did have a dream come true

Disco

Disco…sounds like night lights, music, and fun
No, hold your horses it's just a feathered one
It's my bird an African Grey Parakeet
Whom I have over eighty years to keep

I got him three months past May
Now he is six years old today
Mimicking every sound, he hears
Learning speech year by year

Calling all household names
To him it's just his talking games
He says "f….er" and I say "rass"
Disco makes his own "f….ker rass"

His favorite person of all
Is my daughter "Kai" he always calls
Knock on wood he will say "who"
Tell him your name he might curse at you

Disco a talking wonder bird
New to me I never heard
A bird that talks and lives in a cage
Disco my African Grey will outlive my age

DANVILLE TARDIEL

Down On The Rock

Down on the rock of wood and water
Life threatens human disaster
Limitless procreation
Leading to ultimate life destruction

Was a nice and peaceful land
Back in time blown away in the sand
Haven for perverts and abusers
Not only indigenous but also intruders

Down in the land of wood and water
The light gets dark, and the dark gets darker
'Twas once out of many one people
Now out of many too many people

Leaders lead blind
Masses follow behind
No one look at tomorrow
No one see the impending sorrow

Schools on shift system children to booth
They have nothing only their youth
Freedom and unethical indulgences
Numb their collective senses

Somehow there must be an intervention
To halt and offer a measure of salvation
The system is poised for self-implosion
If this life continues without any aversion

So, relax and ease your mind
Can't turn back the hands of time
But slow down the pace of life
Jamaica don't deserve this strive

DANVILLE TARDIEL

Earth Soil

Soil of the Earth
Supreme mother of birth
Turning and tilling since the start of time
Taking the roots and giving up the vine
Most times wearing a grassy face
You're always present in every place

You carpet the earth in and out
Up and down and all about
Clinging on to backs of rocks
Bearing trees on mountain tops
Variant in colors so true
Like all the elements on top of you

Wind, rain, sunshine, or snow
Always allowing the path to grow
Host of life on earth as we know
Reaping the harvest of what we sow
The genius of life we can't deny
Companion in time as mankind passes by

East West Heritage

My soul had sailed the seven seas
Even before I was conceived to be
My people came from the far east
India, after the death of the slave beast
Contracted on indenture
Seeking new adventure

They came upon an Island spice
Jamaica, my home my paradise
Long hair light skin not Caucasian
More Negroid of Indian persuasion
Born and bred in Jamaica West Indies
Original heritage from the East Indies

Second generation Jamaican
Ancestors had no time to plan
By chance upon the winds of trade
They came to love the life they made
White, yellow, black, and brown West Indian
Out of many Peoples one Jamaican

Father

Father, Mother, all in one
All I know since my life began
Daddy might be my first word spoken
Mother left Father heartbroken
My dad passed on my late teen year
Natural causes took him out of here
Taught me all I needed to know
To live and strive, come rain or snow
To make it against all odds
Was the wisdom of my dad
Now on my life's plateau
I worship my dad, the only parent I knew

First Smile, First Mile

When your life leaves all its' troubles at your feet
Not what you expect to meet
Then what?
You brace yourself and commit to that
All the unexpected rigmaroles
Stand firm and deal with them all

It's a picture of your life on wheels
No exonerations no appeals
You take or leave one day at a time
Sooner or later, you see the line
It's easy when you already know
What the cause lurking down below

My life is miles away
I will love her till my last day
Am breaking down one step from decay
I love my baby, my first born, first smile make my day
Please stay for a while
Let me finish the first mile

DANVILLE TARDIEL

Forbidden Love

Gather your thoughts chase your dreams
People in love forever it seems
Back and forth across the horizon
Never losing momentum never out of reason
It is eternal, a wish, a rhyme, a white dove
It is the sweet taste of forbidden love

People of all assortments like to partake
Love to love never can forsake
The dreams of youth and carefree attractions
Tumbling in a sea of emotional concoctions
Living under shadows of a dark and stormy cloud
Quiet…shh, the voice of forbidden love never speaks loud

Relationships as real as the flakes of snow
Tons of emotions to those who know
Look, listen, use your imagination
No one wants to tell you any confession
Twisted lives born of lust for the flesh
Forbidden love never old always fresh

Peek-a-boo pick a view
Forbidden love waits for you
Takes you on a journey of sex and ecstasy
Like a bad drug in your vein, satisfy your fantasy
False pretense no pleasure no pain
Forbidden love soaks through like a shower of rain

DANVILLE TARDIEL

Fork In The Road Of Life

Life stands still at the edge of conflict
The crossroads at where the road split
Flip a coin pick a straw
Shuffle the deck make a draw
One way or the other you must go
When the cap fit you will know

One life to live no guarantees
Falling apart almost on your knees
Traveled long roads lived deep dreams
Done many things many more it seems
Bounty of life things you really need
Never compete never over greed

One life story to tell
Whether in heaven or in hell

———

The words come out the same
In this life no shame to the game
Cloudy mind feelings up and down
Keep on trucking till you come around

At the Fork you pick your way
Looking for someone, something, a brighter day
Moving on
Resilience strong
Through desolation through pain
Getting there sunshine or rain

Hold on to your hole card for sure
When life's disregard knocks on your door
Passion, pain, or what you forgot
Rhythm, rhyme, ecstasy or not
Make the choice live strong and long
Fork in the road of life will be long gone

Friends

Friends for life
Famous line for man and wife
Not this time
Just two friends on the timeline
Memories that never fade
Even before the first grade

Living in each other's existence
Always aware of each other's presence
Over time past half a century
Friendship strong never weary
Roads we travel roads yet to see
We both know what is to be must be

A time to live and a time to die
Friends for life you and I
Much lost time to regain
Much happiness much pain
Two prints on the sands of time

———

Friendship

I find myself thinking about you at the most random times
Seems like every day you're on my mind
I'm sorry I never told you how much you meant to me
Looks like I am the shyest a person can be
But if there was a way, I could bring you back to life
God knows I would do it in the blink of an eye
I will never forget the good times we've shared
Or the cute things you'd do to show me you cared
Although we are apart, my dear friend
You will always be in my heart until we meet again

DANVILLE TARDIEL

I Am Crying

I am crying am about to breakdown
I am dying 'cause I can't hear a sound
I am screaming but there's no one around
Must be dreaming about my old hometown

I was born and raised in Jamaica
Then I find myself in America
I lost my mother up in Canada
Where she once lived with my older brother

Living full time in the U.S.
Dealing every day with the color test
Unlike the Island where I come from
Always wondering where you belong

So, I'll be crying about to breakdown
I am dying 'cause I can't hear a sound
I am screaming but there's no one around
Must be dreaming about my old hometown

Sweet reggae music let it calm my soul
Island foods I might never grow old
Till I reach my limit my natural life span
I will always be a Jamaica man

In Dreams I See

Tonight, I sleep my normal sleep my normal bed
In supine posture my normal pillow beneath my head
Then my subconscious creep
Deep in my sleep
In places I know very well
Familiar faces I can tell

Saw them before
All in the same place for sure
See them again more than one maybe ten
Contemplating the lives of men
Then speak the essence of those gone before
Set the record straight open the door

Tell the story true from us to you
Let them understand what you already knew
We herald the end with dignity and love
No hard feelings, on the wings of a dove
Some may weep some may cheer

DANVILLE TARDIEL

For all we know others beware

The deeds of those who speculate
Leave it all at the metal gate
Take the ammunition you need clear the way
Blaze a trail, tell the story, before life's decay
Clarify to those who seek the truth
We are happy as we ever were in our youth

In The Ghetto Where We Echo

All my life I've been listening
To the sound of people talking
The birds in the trees
The wind in the leaves
Then one day my friend picked up the mic and said

This is the ghetto
Where we echo
It's where we came from
Its where we belong
Live your life and be strong
Cause nothing can ever go wrong

All my life I've been looking
Not knowing what it is that I'm seeking
All I know is what's in me
Are the things I feel and see

DANVILLE TARDIEL

This is the ghetto
Where we echo
It's where we came from
Its where we belong
Live your life and be strong
Cause nothing can ever go wrong

Indian Summer

Several months past summer
The breeze feels stronger
As it rustles through the trees
Dropping multicolored leaves
Redecorating the matted green grass
Like a huge mosaic on canvas
Enchanting, penetrating the mind
Like a warm breeze in the summertime
Indian Summer in the Folklore
After which follows winter for sure
The apertures get larger as the leaves fall
Sooner or later only sticks standing tall

Inflamed Heart

Last night in dreams I killed you
I saw you crying I know you hurt too
I am the one who escalate
Hoping nothing was too late
Cause I bear a certain pain
I begot you under life's refrain
You got me 100% in your vein
Maybe that is why you remain un-stain
I love you much too much to complain
So, I pen you these lines before I go insane
Daughter of mine every inch on time
Will never hurt you in your life or mine
Forgive my deeds I love you no lie
That will never change till the day I die
My other the inveterate pain
Will never stop till I go insane
Now I'm hurt and torn apart
I'm living day by day with an inflamed heart

I Am Brentwood

I am Brentwood

A town where I have lived my whole life

A diverse neighborhood

Filled with violence and strife

Gang wars and crimes are occasional

In different parts of the town

All of this conflict is nonsensical

Is it really fun being a clown?

On the upside, our school system is one of the best

Just the other day, a friend of mine was declared an Intel Semi-Finalist

I love to meet people from different cultures

And find those who share my own

My friends help shape my future

And discover things once unknown

I don't know if or when I'll leave this place

But one thing is for sure

I will always cherish the memories I've made

For they are the greatest cure

My only hope is that Brentwood will soon see better days

And that all the violence will transition into a more peaceful phase.

Jamaica

Jamaica, land of wood and water
When you visit nothing seems to matter
A Caribbean spice Island
A beautiful place, blue waters, and white sand

Beaches stretching over seven miles long
Jamaica, like a sweet summer song
People travel from far far lands
To enjoy hot sun and trade winds

From England even the Netherlands
They be jamming to the reggae songs
Island in the sun
Spring break, magnitude of fun

Jamaican sweet coconut water
Best on the menu conch maybe lobster
Add some rum and let it spill
Whatever it takes to get your fill

Mango, apple, and June plum
Red stripe beer and white rum
Trade winds summer breeze
Jamaica, no problem, always at ease

Life's Aftermath

The passing of one tired soul
Left us in a sea of emotions out of control
Finding secret thoughts and aspirations
Numb minds and negative vibrations
Clouds of visionary unspoken salutations
Intonations of voices filled unlikely emotions

As we fumble over others bequeath
We hover over the path, the aftermath of life equals death
The stormy sea the raging waves
Left us lost in a confusing maze
In the midst of it all stands one strong and tall
As it pinches our soul and beckons our call

From the depths the denizen rise
Calming the waves and tendering the tides
Reaching in vain for the other side
As death speaks up, it's the aftermath of life
In life we trace the tracks of our dreams
As we heed the roaring thunder and crack at the seams

Seeping mixed emotions of good and bad
Living in the slumber of the lives we had

DANVILLE TARDIEL

Forsaken not forgotten are the days of our lives

Breaking away day by day out of sight of our eyes

Then the stage is empty, no more worry, no more fret

Then we meet and understand, the aftermath of life equals death

Lost

"Enjoy it while it lost"
"Live life no matter what the cost"
Famous words of a known acquaintance
Euphoric anthem in better circumstance
No respect for mother or child
Schemes and dreams that went wild

Chants "enjoy it while it lost"
Always embracing and reinstating the past
Easy come easy go he say
Tomorrow just another day
Never look in the future ahead
Till one day the mother was dead

Inheritance came no surprise
Still refuse to open his eyes
Went on a spree uptown debonair
Spending money in expensive atmosphere
Suddenly, rock bottom sets in reality calls
Homeless and broke like a bum he falls

Lunacy

I see the moon by willow light
Staring at the bleak of night
In her unroyal pomp and state
She seems to think her sallow face
Which has misled us age by age
In the thought that she's loves' aid
Requires no makeup to disguise
The crust upon her jaundiced eyes
The shaft unleashed by Romeo
Was most appro po
That she "old moon" was sick and green
But now am sure she feels quite mean
The puppet that mankind was deemed
That is in sense of small extreme
Once showed itself to be
Dancing to her phony airs of mystery
Has now found joy in dancing
Over her curvy rocky head…moon walking
This poem written in lunar rhyme
Is just another moon-caused crime

Lust For Love

It was a burning love at the start
Cupids' arrow penetrates the heart
It smoked, cindered, and flame
Romantic ash and a love child, is all that remain
Two people in love not for sure
Distant chronology love could not endure
Love and lives that spans
One maybe two generations

It might have been love
Two wishes on a snow-white dove
But its' over now
We've lost it some how
Extra familial interference
Incestuous urges encumbrance
Banging on the wall
Love vibrations eventually fall

Was good till it's gone
Three lives must move on
The umbilical cord is cut
The door to love is shut
Now in the gloom

DANVILLE TARDIEL

Of this empty room

I sit and wait

Upon this everlasting faith

Man Fibe Free

Man, fibe free since the 17th century

Man, fibe free don't ask me

Man, fibe free no bending knees

Man, fibe free now ask me please

This is the new generation

And we don't forget our original creation

One voice, one love, one heart

One people of many we will start

World dominance is what we claim

Ain't no power bigger than our claim to fame

Man, fibe free since the 17th century

Man, fibe free don't ask me

Man, fibe free no bending knees

Man, fibe free now ask me please

New age, new living, in white no crime

Tell all the world it's about time

People should live together in harmony

Like flowers in the garden one destiny

Different root, different pedals a pretty sight to see

Man, fibe free since the 17th century

Man, fibe free don't ask me

Man, fibe free no bending knees

Man, fibe free now ask me please

DANVILLE TARDIEL

Miracle

It was a while ago you smiled at me
Fresh out the womb like a miracle to be
Now you've grown in brains and beauty
Ready to take on the world and its bounty
First child born in a loving bond
Sky is the limit achieving above and beyond
Rolling with the waves of life's' surprises
Never giving up or giving in to distracting vices
Two decades and half to this penmanship
You never waver on your goals no matter the hardship
Confident and sure to reach life's' pinnacle
Four, twenty-three, ninety-four was the day of a true miracle

Momma

A woman of class and distinction
We love you ... We your spawned generation
You gave so much of your life to us
Ever since youth we learn to trust
Tonight, we relish the past
You gave your everything up to the last
For the years we lived and spent with you
Hopes and dreams did come true
Now we miss you, your voice, your face
Indelible moments in time and space
Our past, our present, and our future we undertake
Our love for you we'll never forsake
Time goes on time will fly
Today we live tomorrow we die
All we are is what we take
We love you Momma ... See you at Heavens' gate

DANVILLE TARDIEL

Morbidity

Gone are the days of thinking roses
No longer the need for counting daises
People, places, and all kinds of races
Fighting for power in all different stages
No love no care for each other
Kicking and biting trying to kill one another

Structures break down humanity crumble
Everyone waits for the other to stumble
Bearing down bad will and ill influences
Destroying each other with evil processes
Selfishness reigns in all their hearts
Breeding nothing but terror and morbid thoughts

Searching life's scroll in this time and age
Confusion, competition, and frustration set the stage
People lost in extreme technology
Losing all measure of true mortality
Looking no further than the eye can see
Swimming…drowning in a sea of morbidity

Morning Twilight

Open my eyes this August morning
In the twilight of the dawning
Dim light piercing through the apertures
Of tree leaves dancing overtures
Reflecting on my windowpane
Like Fairies in a musical fairytale
I laid and watched the Fairies dance
Could be asleep maybe a trance

But as the hot ball rise
It was no surprise
To see the subtle change
As my shutter turned into a live stage
Now fully lit
As the sunshine hit
I see shadows of tree leaves bright
Dancing in the morning twilight

The sun rose high
Golden light floods the sky
The stage went bare
No leaves no Fairies left there
The spectacle subsides
In the morning sunrise
The magic was gone much too soon
As the morning sun greets the noon

Mother

Dear Mother,
As I write you this line
It's too late to rewind the hands of time
Can't say never maybe too late

Cause you're somewhere knocking on heavens' gate
This is the stone abandoned and refused
The head corner stone now being used
Now we sever the ties that bind

Only memories will be left behind
Put all burdens on the river side
Awaiting the rising of the tide
Like a drop of rain in the ocean

My teardrop in the sea of emotion
Countless nights I struggle with this thought
Countless battles in my mind I fought
Now the rain is gone no more confusion

Can see clear through all disillusion
Must do this impossible task
And answer all the questions you ask
Must dissolve the illusion

And make an amicable conclusion

Mountains Of Jamaica

The mountains run from east to west
And in the Island look the best
In the east the highest
And in the west the lowest
They never seem to be a far
When you are driving in a car

The mountains home of the Maroons
Rebel slaves gone too soon
Western hills of the Cockpit country
Rebel slaves build their army
Countering the English cavalry
First step in the war on slavery

Beautiful mountains of the Isle
Echo sweet rhythms Jamaican style
Peaks and valleys and rolling hills
Rain and lightning and thunder fills
Oh! Beautiful mountains of the Isle
Upon your peak there is a smile

DANVILLE TARDIEL

My Pool Of Thoughts

Home again by the edge of the pool
Familiar feeling like I'm back in school
Trying to read signs and sounds around me
Looking up, down, as far as my eyes could see
Taking notes verse by verse
Taking time as my mind traverse

Looking back, it seems ever since my birth
Nothing stays the same in the heavens or the earth
Changes seem a way of life to be
Today am here tomorrow no one can see
Wrinkles of aging must be
Erasing all signs of puberty

So, I follow as emotions lead
To a place in time, I must concede
To live my life on the path I choose
With pain or passion win or loose
One day I will find at the end of the line
That my life was just a speck in time

Native Son

Native son, son of the soil
No change, nothing can spoil
Patriotic to the bone
Solid as a rock, concrete, even a stone
Land of my birth will never desert
My heart is buried under the earth
For better or worse or whatever to come
One day reunite and become one
Destined to be surrounded by sea
Warm trade winds blowing through me
Saving my soul for future endeavor
Never a butterfly, never a caterpillar

DANVILLE TARDIEL

New York Summer

Summer up north a wonderful season
Everyone outside without a reason
Basking in the light of the burning sun
From morning till evening till the day is done
Even after the phase of the golden sun
Some will be waiting for the moonlight to come
Temperatures will rise
Some will act surprise
Dog days of summer they say
Others will have it no other way
Whatever you choose hot or cold
Just like life the young must grow old

Power Of Addiction

Voices speaking in my head
Asking, where are you? what are you doing? and I said
I'm here in a comfort zone
This is my space, a place I call home
No constraint, no contradiction
It is called the power of addiction

Some say wine, some say rum
Some say bring anything you got come
Some snort up the nose
Some drink till the bar is close
Whatever it is, it's all the same affliction
It is simply the power of addiction

So, we treat this ailing condition night and day
B1, B6, folic acid, multivitamin, or another way
However, we choose
We try to lose
Feelings of anguish and desperation
It is the supreme power of addiction

———

DANVILLE TARDIEL

This is the cry of man from start of time
Before the divine intervention or a line that rhyme
We struggle with life as it beats our cheeks
Looking for a way to release our speech
All that remains is the same sensation
Simply the essence of addiction

We drink of the fruits of the earth
We work with the plants that it birth
Some for the good of life as we know
We live and learn as we grow
However, whatever you take from this rendition
Remember it's dedicated to the power of addiction

Rain

Showers of blessings sometimes we say
One of many thoughts on a rainy day
Getting soaked like a child at play
Some may say rain dance today

Like crystal diamond drops in the sunshine
Never too late for a shower of rain anytime
Two Hydrogen one Oxygen atoms together
Give us rain in our climatic weather

The desert craves it on a parched summers' day
Others are impatient for it to go away
Rain, rain, bless us another day
Is the song of those with time to play

The earth drinks it's sweet molecule
Give back life is the golden rule
Quenching the thirst of all living things
Fueling the circle of life as it spins

Rain, rain, life solution
Element of divine conception
Water, the essence of all that is rain
Rain, the essence of life to sustain

Re-Tired

The end the rainbow
The ribbon in the sky
The golden glow
The eternal high
Now you foreclose
Now see you the light
No more doors can close
No more sleepless night
No more personal industry
No more others personal life takes the day
No more work no more duty
No more worry along the way
Time to live the life you love
Time to live the life you made
Time to sit and watch the dove
Time to sit, chill, and relax under the shade

Reality

Realty is a state of mind
A sliding scale on the timeline
Of life not but a speck in time
Sane or insane for whom the bell chyme
Ever since humanity
Mankind fights with sanity
There is no measure to this emotion
No limits no one point of devotion
Everyone thinks their measure
Is everyone else treasure
Reality like a balance beam
Tips either way for self esteem
We are a lot or a little insane
Whatever stimulates our brain
The mind of man cannot fathom
Reality the same no top no bottom

DANVILLE TARDIEL

Religion Contemplation

Question is what is your Religion?
Pending your region of origin
Your familial denomination
Your answer maybe any variation

For God so love the world
He gave his only son, not a girl
Died on the cross
To find you if you're lost

Praises to Allah
Some say in God's honor
More than one wife
So, they live their lives

Buddha bless you
Cross your legs, meditate true
Burning incense, clear the air
You'll be blessed if you play it fair

Jah Rastafari
Who cares if you live or die?
God is a living man
With the master plan

———

Krishna Krishna
Karma Dharma
From life to death on earth
Born again maybe a rebirth

God of the Universe
Punjab is another verse
Ever expanding
No start no ending

Monotheistic Jew
Say you're the chosen few
In the bosom of Abraham, you are
Represent with a six-point star

Come together in the Bahai
Messengers in a graphic pie
Living in the Omni- prefix
God, Religion, and Humans in the mix

Cao Dai
From a low to a high
Religious Amnesty of the third Era
Teachings of Saint, Sage, and Buddha

Satanism and Atheist in the mist
All together in one, The Universalist
Out of many one Religion
The Universal principal life lives on

DANVILLE TARDIEL

Semi-Automatic

Put down the matic, the semi-automatic
Life too short boy it might get drastic
Try to walk don't try to run
Live for peace and have some fun
Today you're here tomorrow you're gone
Deep, deep, down under the ground
Put down the matic, the semi-automatic
Life too short boy it might get drastic
Sometimes you up, sometimes you down
Live long enough and you will come around
Fast lane, fast gain, heartache and pain
When the pan drop only yourself to blame
So, put down the matic, the semi-automatic
Life too short boy it might get drastic
On your motor bike crank up and you go
Two-gun kid like you a Django
Riding high ignoring the peace
Then you end up at the foot of the police

———

Shadowy Moon

A shadowy moon pierced the night sky
I stood at the bottom of the stairs watching dark clouds float by
Half a moon like emotions broken
Drifting silent and unspoken
An old song comes to mind
Evoking memories of a better time

"When the moon takes the place of the sun in the sky
I'll call for my girl we'll go walking by"
This is the twilight of life emotions run high
Bad things good things they born then they die
Like the drifting dark clouds souls pass on high
Across the intermittent smile of the moon in the sky

Souls sail in the night if you pay attention
Wind drift silhouettes no shape no dimension
One for me one for you
One for all who pass through
They all dissipate in the distance
As we all do at the end of our existence

DANVILLE TARDIEL

Spring In Winter...The Brooklyn Botanical Gardens

'Twas a cold and snowy day
During the season jolly and gay
Was a place warm the only one
Heat by the winter tropical sun

Any means through this contemporary jungle
On a mission so humble
To collect copy from the green house in the borough
To pen these lines for tomorrow

Roads filled with traffic slow
Accidents everywhere you go
Snow piled high to the sky
Plows trying to move it by

Destination after a while
Sights and smells make you smile
Transports to another place
A rose garden at your embrace

Scenes and aromas touch you deeply
Memories of childhood fantasy
Days and nights dreams in slumber
Poinsettias red in a warm December

DANVILLE TARDIEL

Spring Peek

Another year, another stage
Another point on your age
Wind still outside the window
Leaves dance in suspended limbo
Birds chirping
Sweet sounds in early morning
Ready to nest and mate
Phenomena of the hands of faith
Grassy stage damp with dew
Awaiting sunshine to dry through
Come the light summer is near
Get ready spring is in the air

Starting Ground

One recent visit to the starting ground
Unfamiliar faces, places, and sound
Out of touch with all that's real
Stupid numbness no one can feel

The wind, the rain, not even the sun
Tantalized, obsessed with the feel of the gun
Stealing and killing escapade
No longer is there comfort in the shade

New generation dumb and mindless
Minding and watching others business
Waiting for the window, the stroke of faith
Ready to pounce and perpetrate

Guns on the run all over town
Authority waiting to pitch them down
One by one like dominoes
Is there an end? Is there a stop? No one knows.

DANVILLE TARDIEL

Sun On The Run

The sun is on the run
Winter the Fall, soon become
Colliding with Trade Winds storm maker
Still better than an earth shaker
In the Tropic of Cancer will be
Tropical storms that threaten the sea

Sun migrates to the deep south
In the Tropic of Capricorn or somewhere about
Two mid-summers in the Earths waistline
People enjoy every year, every time
In between lies a tropical kingdom
People travel far just to get some

Drinking and eating exotic menu
Always offered in every venue
The northern and southern solstice of the earth
Puts the sun in its Zenith from birth
The northern hemisphere eagerly awaits its return
For warm summer nights and daytime sunburn

Sunshine

Even in the Wintertime, it's a pleasure to see
Light beams staring down on me
The hottest spot in the Galaxy
A ball of burning gas energy
Shooting rays of sunshine
Illuminating blanket in the daytime
At nightfall
The sky seems tall
No sun to mark the center
Only the moon on the perimeter
Reflecting residual sunshine
Revolving rotating like the hands of time
Animal screams
Plants awaken from their dreams
Humans start circadian rhythm
Much warmth like the sunshine within
Childish exuberance "oh what a bright and sunny day"
Sunshine more time to work and play

DANVILLE TARDIEL

Sweet Home Tune

If I could walk there, I would run
By moonlight maybe sun
To the place where I belong
West Jamaica, take me home
Screaming through the air
On a demon that I fear

Climbing, it's a very long stair
Whatever it takes I must get there
Looking out the window
Nothing moves, only sunlight on my eyebrow
Above the clouds, above the rain
Moving faster than a subway train

Look right look left, no one seem to care
Then reality sets in and you know you're nowhere
You are a passenger, yes you are
Traveling very fast and very far
Riding on a high

Wondering if you live or die
Floating on thin air
Pretending you don't care

___

Riding on the risk of life, no control

Living on the edge of dreams in your soul

So, keep the wind on your back, flow on through

Sweet home west Jamaica, coming home to you

DANVILLE TARDIEL

Sweet Reggae Music

Sweet reggae music, designed to rock your bone
Sweet reggae music, coming out of Jam down
Sweet reggae music, wake up and tell the town
Sweet reggae music, playing it all night long
First it was the wicked Ska, leave you lightheaded
Then comes the cool and deadly, the one Rocksteady
Now lend me your drum, lend me your base
Give me little space, let me wine up my waist
Sweet reggae music, play for my brother man
Sweet reggae music, play it all day long
Sweet reggae music, play it loud and strong
Sweet reggae music, play for me when I am gone

The Glass

Back once more at the glass

Holding on a moment that could last

Sunshine floods my view

Wind, no rain, I see clear through

Holding on the edge of a lifetime

Memories all sublime

This glass, I see through an open hole

No mirrors to the soul

Just an impassable path

A piece of wall, contain me and my thought

Looking out at twigs for trees

No sway, just a shake in the breeze

Looking out this glass, wishing I could go

Far away moments, from the cold wind that blow

To the land of my birth, no snow all sun

Any day now, it's time for me to run

So, I look at the pretty sunlight

Hoping for better sweet dreams tonight

DANVILLE TARDIEL

The Palm Coast Toast

Raise your glass to Palm Coast
This is it the final toast
To a life of work well done
The only place under the sun
To live the dreams of boredom
A little place, a little Kingdom

After a life of toil and stress
This is the time to relax and rest
In Palm Coast near the ocean blue
It will be there waiting for you
Come one come all come anytime
Come see the final stop on the timeline

After all the work is done
Retirement, like the setting sun
In Palm Coast it will be better
Any day, any time, any weather
Slow pacing time is the essence
Time to relish close ones in your presence

———

Palmed yards and pine trees
So many leaves to catch the breeze
Warm off the ocean shore
Who could ask for anything more?
Summer breeze blowing through the mind
Palm Coast, the final stop in time

DANVILLE TARDIEL

The Pool

The scent of chlorine fills the air
Like a fresh wash of whites from your Frigidaire
Clear through to the bottom I see
In a puddle of water taller than me

It's a pool, man made
Echoes a certain accolade
A pride a joy
A kid's toy

Various dimensional body of water
Various depths and square area
Swimmers and all, always welcome
Always a child's water Kingdom

The pool a pleasant invite
On days when the temperature spikes
I embrace this wonder of man
To have a pool of water on dry land

The Rx Milieu

There is a place of all work and no play
A place to do, not a place to stay
Anticipating the moment to the end
Never knowing what waits around the bend
People in a bundle
Some hyped, some humble

Mixed thoughts mental conditions
Minds in crises treatment ambitions
Mild, moderate, and severe
Calm, quiet, even unaware
Time passes slowly by
Life's emotions flying high

Separate lives mixed in one place
Hard to read signs on the face
Many people, one mind set
Some lose it, some better yet
All travel this familiar pathway
Some make it out, others tend to stay

DANVILLE TARDIEL

This place healthy, therapeutic, a safe house
Still not good for man or mouse
Compromised minds at work
Some stay calm, some go berserk
Still, they come one by one and quite a few
To the Psych unit, the safe house, it's the therapeutic Milieu

The Window

Standing here in limbo
Staring out the window
Looking at a phenomenon
Born of another land
Strange climatic condition
Rain down white stuff on the horizon

Looking out the window
Searching for a rainbow
None in sight
Neither day, nor night
Waiting out the flow
It's the white stuff they call snow

Staring out the window, as far as I can see
Nothing resembles the land that brought me
I see trees without leaves
Flat roofs in the breeze
Buildings in the distant…High rise
Leaving me shocked and mesmerize

DANVILLE TARDIEL

What is this place I see through the glass?
Cold, ice, frigid, how long will it last
What is this place cold as hell?
Not the feelings, it's emotions I can tell
Smoking chimneys, fire in the hearth
I must go I need a brand-new start

Still standing here staring out the window
Seven years, seven long more years to go
Wondering if by choice
I might make it to paradise
No one knows, that's how the story goes
Until then, I watch as the snow flows

Tropical Sunset

Have you ever seen a tropical sunset?
Many have come my way, no pictures yet
The sun, like a gentle yellow ball
Dipping in the sea as it falls
Then the golden hue lines the sky
As people on the beach go walking by
Snap shots like crazy
Everyone in a picture frenzy
It's always a sight to see
The great yellow ball falling in the sea
If you never seen this phenomenon
Then it's time that you should travel on

DANVILLE TARDIEL

Tweet, Tweet, Tweet

Sitting by the pool, my morning retreat
Better than the beach, no sand on my feet
Listening to the sound of water
Suddenly, "tweet, tweet, tweet," baby bird cry for hunger
Up above me as I rest
A well woven bird's nest
Baby birds inside cried, tweet, tweet, tweet
Mother bird answered, a sound so sweet
Like a note from a musical instrument
Baby birds seem to know what it meant
The tweets got softer
Now I can hear the flow of pool water
Taking me back to my quiet retreat
listening to the sounds of nature, so sweet
If you interpret what they say
It could be, what a wonderful day
And if you ask what they do
It would be nothing … Just like you

Waster

Around me lives a certain man
Whose ways I don't understand
Lays his head down with no delay
Wakes up late every day
Sits for hours staring into space
No signs of emotions on his face

Looks lost and depressed
Like someone in deep distress
No work, no play
Nothing to do, any given day
No claim to his name, now or later
This man is the ultimate waster

In speech he is adamant in disorientation
About life and it's expectation
Just like a vegetable waiting to rot
Or nocturnal creatures to attack
Refusing to move in any direction
To fulfill his purpose on this land
Lives his life in severe limitation

DANVILLE TARDIEL

Rationalizing on other people's action
Subscribing to life's lazy recluse
Opportunities he conveniently refuse
Sure, signs of a distorted mentality
Living in a world of a wasted reality

Where I'm From

by Katherine Tardiel

I'm from the mini melting pot of Long Island
from the side of town where fruits line the streets
from big backyards and tall trees
from the cherry, pear, peach, and plum trees.
I'm from the booming sound of music and the smell of family gatherings
from the panting of Rusty and Wishbone
from the sparkling blue water enclosed with a cement frame
from the battery powered vehicles running over the grass.
I'm from the dancing bundle of feathers with a loud potty mouth
from the young and fierce little Doberman
who showed up when one chapter of my life closed.
I'm from a heritage known for its tropical bliss and wondrous landscapes
from the relaxing reggae music and flavorful cuisine
from the beautiful sunsets, the humid climate, and the charming people.
I'm from a close and loving family of three
from two parents who do not spoil me and love me unconditionally
from close friends who share my company
And I adore all of these things, for they have made me who I am.

DANVILLE TARDIEL

Winter

In the bitterness of our winters
The ice is not all that splinters
The cracking and craving doesn't end
With the advent of the spring my friend
With the Forsythia comes life trailing
Vibrant colorful flowering
Its trailing glory is but a jest
Beauty is from rose to fire to a bird's nest
Fall sits in its precedence
Winter is no recompense
Slip the deck, roll the dice
It must come up pure white ice

Work Dilemma

Some people say work, some say why
Some say either you do or either you die
Still, we work come what may
Looking forward to a better day
At the end of the rainbow
For all we know

Some hidden treasure, maybe a pot of gold
Some find the futile end when the hand gets fold
Life is given and must be taken
You must know when to hold and when to forsaken
Punching the clock is not easy at all
Some people crumble, some heed the call

Work is a given from way back when
It's up to us to break or bend
Life is not a gamble; you must know what to hold
The deck is in your hand, deal it, find your pot of gold
Work is a dilemma, we all know that it is
Whether you like what you do or do it with ease
One day you hope to find
Some happiness, some peace of mind
Somewhere over the hill on top of the mount

DANVILLE TARDIEL

You hope to accomplish on your own account

A place in the sun where all life begun

Away from work dilemma forever will be gone

CPSIA information can be obtained
at www.ICGtesting.com
Printed in the USA
LVHW080155140421
684463LV00016B/373